Serenity

Contemplation

Balance   Reflection

Composure   ★

★   Self-Possession

Contentment

A World of Mindfulness

From the **Editors**
& Illustrators
of **Pajama Press**

It's not surprising that **mindfulness** and meditation are being taught even in kindergartens and preschools today. These tools help children concentrate, manage their emotions, and stay resilient through the evolving changes in their lives. My creative team and I wanted to craft a book that centers the mindful experience of young children as they tune into all their senses and emotions.

This book celebrates the art from several of our award-winning illustrators but also features some exceptional new artists for you to discover. The pages ahead highlight children finding their calm in all sorts of different ways. This stunning collection of art, paired with a sensitive text, evokes peace, warmth, and hope.

Our beautiful collaborative picture book is dedicated to all children struggling to navigate our uncertain world.

Gail

Gail Winskill, Publisher
Pajama Press

I am here. I know who I am. I breathe in the smell of fresh-cut grass and it fills my lungs with energy.

When I run, my muscles
stretch and I feel powerful.

The sun is warm on my face. It is millions of miles away, but we are still connected.

I can hear birds and breezes and a dog barking. Even with my eyes closed, I know where I am.

When I blow bubbles, they shine with rainbows. It's nice to think of nothing else as I watch them float away.

Sometimes my mind is like a mixed-up swirling snowstorm. It isn't right or wrong—it's just how I feel.

Bad feelings are like cold snow melting in my hand. I feel them...I acknowledge them... and eventually they are gone.

Sometimes it's fun to be a little bit scared.

Quiet things can be thrilling too, like
the smell of a brand-new book, and
the smoothness of its pages, and the
sound they make turning over.

I feel important when
I make things with my
own hands.

Cookies fresh from the oven
taste like happy memories.

My favorite pajamas are soft against my skin, and my sheets feel cozy and clean.

I know who I am. I am someone
who sees, smells, hears, tastes, and
feels the world around me. I know
where I am. I am here.

Use your senses. Find your calm.

Mindfulness means taking time to pay close attention to how we feel. It can help calm down our bodies and our brains. It also helps us concentrate and solve problems.

Breathe in

Breathe out

You are here

First published in Canada and the United States in 2020

Text copyright © 2020 Erin Alladin
Illustration copyright © 2020 Tara Anderson, Aino Anto, Rebecca Bender, Andrea Blinick, Tamara Campeau, Suzanne Del Rizzo, Amélie Dubois, Gabrielle Grimard, Sue Macartney, Carmen Mok, Emma Pedersen, Scot Ritchie, Miki Sato, François Thisdale
This edition copyright © 2020 Pajama Press Inc.
This is a first edition.

10 9 8 7 6 5 4 3 2 1

www.pajamapress.ca info@pajamapress.ca

Canada Council Conseil des arts
for the Arts du Canada

ONTARIO ARTS COUNCIL
CONSEIL DES ARTS DE L'ONTARIO
an Ontario government agency
un organisme du gouvernement de l'Ontario

Canadä

The publisher gratefully acknowledges the support of the Canada Council for the Arts and the Ontario Arts Council for its publishing program. We acknowledge the financial support of the Government of Canada through the Canada Book Fund (CBF) for our publishing activities.

Library and Archives Canada Cataloguing in Publication

Title: A world of mindfulness / from the editors & illustrators of Pajama Press.
Names: Alladin, Erin, 1989- writer of added text. | Pajama Press Inc., issuing body.
Description: First edition. | Text by Erin Alladin.
Identifiers: Canadiana 20200262114 | ISBN 9781772781380 (hardcover)
Subjects: LCSH: Mindfulness (Psychology)—Pictorial works—Juvenile literature. | LCSH: Mindfulness (Psychology)—Juvenile literature.
Classification: LCC BF637.M56 W67 2020 | DDC j158.1/30222—dc23

Publisher Cataloging-in-Publication Data (U.S.)

Names: Alladin, Erin, 1989-, editor.

Title: A World of Mindfulness / from the editors & illustrators of Pajama Press.

Description: Toronto, Ontario Canada : Pajama Press, 2020. | Summary: "A series of statements describe common sensory experiences, including the warmth of the sun, the sight of rainbow-hued bubbles, the smell of grass, and the taste of warm cookies. Meditative in tone, the statements connect the speaker's physical senses to their sense of self. Each spread is illustrated by a different artist. Back matter about mindfulness completes the text" -- Provided by publisher.
Identifiers: ISBN 978-1-77278-138-0 (hardcover)
Subjects: LCSH: Mindfulness (Psychology) -- Juvenile literature. | Senses and sensation – Juvenile literature. | Self-consciousness (Awareness) – Juvenile literature. | BISAC: JUVENILE NONFICTION / Health & Daily Living / Mindfulness & Meditation. | JUVENILE NONFICTION / Social Topics / Emotions & Feelings.
Classification: LCC BF637.M56A453 |DDC 158.13 – dc23

Cover and book design—Rebecca Bender

Manufactured by Qualibre Inc./Print Plus
Printed in China

Pajama Press Inc.
181 Carlaw Ave. Suite 251 Toronto, Ontario Canada, M4M 2S1

Distributed in Canada by UTP Distribution
5201 Dufferin Street Toronto, Ontario Canada, M3H 5T8

Distributed in the U.S. by Ingram Publisher Services
1 Ingram Blvd. La Vergne, TN 37086, USA

Calmness ★

Stillness

Awareness

Mindfulness

★

Peace of Mind

Tranquility

Harmony ★